HAL LEONARD
GUITAR METHOD

ACOUSTIC GUITAR SONGS

SECOND EDITION

ISBN 978-1-4950-9796-6

7777 W. BLUEMOUND RD. P.O. BOX 13819 MILWAUKEE, WI 53213

Visit Hal Leonard Online at
www.halleonard.com

Guitar Notation Legend

THE MUSICAL STAFF shows pitches and rhythms and is divided by bar lines into measures. Pitches are named after the first seven letters of the alphabet.

TABLATURE graphically represents the guitar fingerboard. Each horizontal line represents a string, and each number represents a fret.

Notes:

Strings:

4th string, 2nd fret | 1st & 2nd strings open, played together | open D chord

HALF-STEP BEND: Strike the note and bend up 1/2 step.

WHOLE-STEP BEND: Strike the note and bend up one step.

GRACE NOTE BEND: Strike the note and bend up as indicated. The first note does not take up any time.

SLIGHT (MICROTONE) BEND: Strike the note and bend up 1/4 step.

BEND AND RELEASE: Strike the note and bend up as indicated, then release back to the original note. Only the first note is struck.

PRE-BEND: Bend the note as indicated, then strike it.

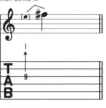

VIBRATO: The string is vibrated by rapidly bending and releasing the note with the fretting hand.

PALM MUTING: The note is partially muted by the pick hand lightly touching the string(s) just before the bridge.

HAMMER-ON: Strike the first (lower) note with one finger, then sound the higher note (on the same string) with another finger by fretting it without picking.

PULL-OFF: Place both fingers on the notes to be sounded. Strike the first note and without picking, pull the finger off to sound the second (lower) note.

LEGATO SLIDE: Strike the first note and then slide the same fret-hand finger up or down to the second note. The second note is not struck.

SHIFT SLIDE: Same as legato slide, except the second note is struck.

TRILL: Very rapidly alternate between the notes indicated by continuously hammering on and pulling off.

TAPPING: Hammer ("tap") the fret indicated with the pick-hand index or middle finger and pull off to the note fretted by the fret hand.

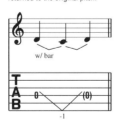

NATURAL HARMONIC: Strike the note while the fret-hand lightly touches the string directly over the fret indicated.

PINCH HARMONIC: The note is fretted normally and a harmonic is produced by adding the edge of the thumb or the tip of the index finger of the pick hand to the normal pick attack.

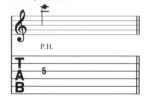

TREMOLO PICKING: The note is picked as rapidly and continuously as possible.

VIBRATO BAR DIVE AND RETURN: The pitch of the note or chord is dropped a specified number of steps (in rhythm) then returned to the original pitch.

VIBRATO BAR SCOOP: Depress the bar just before striking the note, then quickly release the bar.

VIBRATO BAR DIP: Strike the note and then immediately drop a specified number of steps, then release back to the original pitch.

Additional Musical Definitions

(accent) • Accentuate note (play it louder)

(staccato) • Play the note short

D.S. al Coda • Go back to the sign (𝄋), then play until the measure marked *"To Coda"*, then skip to the section labelled *"Coda."*

D.C. al Fine • Go back to the beginning of the song and play until the measure marked *"Fine"* (end).

Fill • Label used to identify a brief melodic figure which is to be inserted into the arrangement.

N.C. • No Chord

 • Repeat measures between signs.

 • When a repeated section has different endings, play the first ending only the first time and the second ending only the second time.

About a Girl

Words and Music by Kurt Cobain

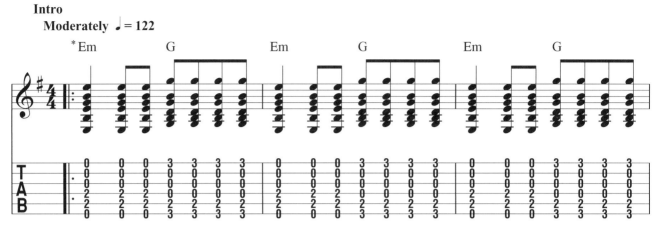

*To match original recording, tune down 1/2 step.

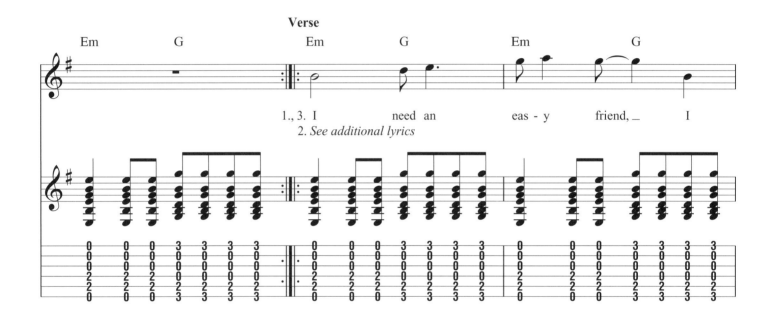

1., 3. I need an eas-y friend, _ I
2. *See additional lyrics*

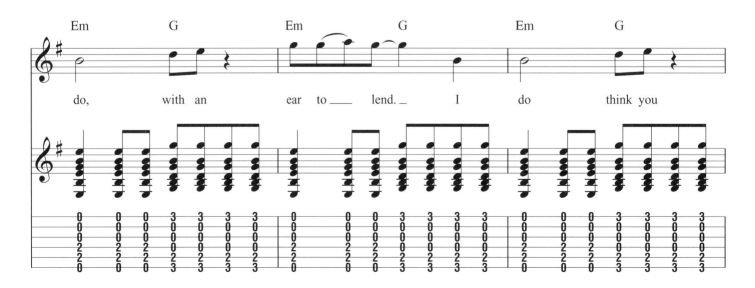

do, with an ear to ___ lend. _ I do think you

Guitar Solo

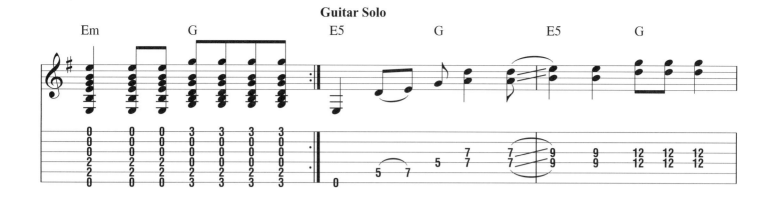

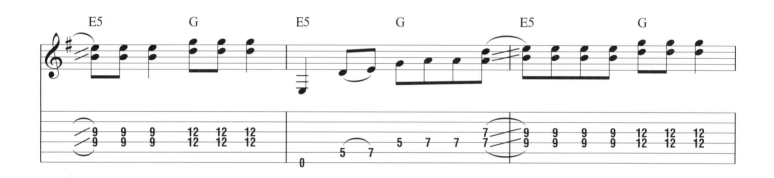

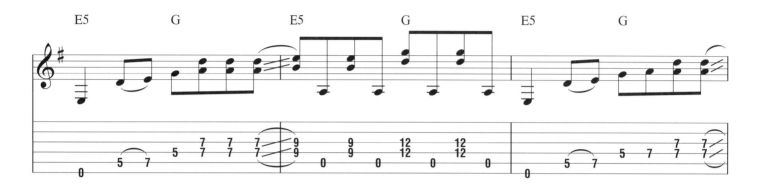

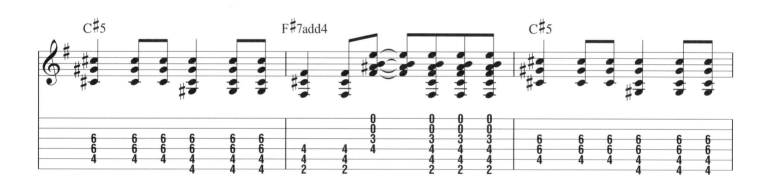

D.C. al Coda
(no repeats)

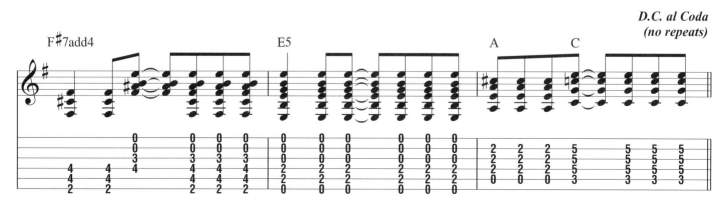

Coda

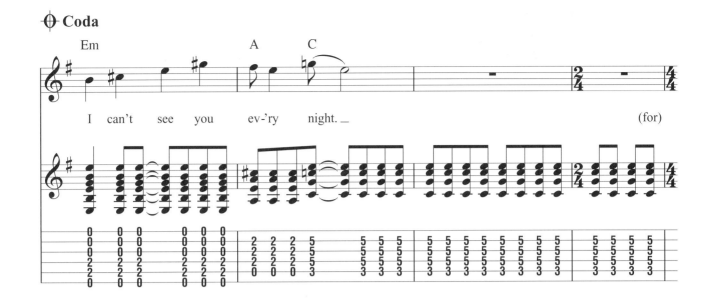

I can't see you ev'ry night. ___ (for)

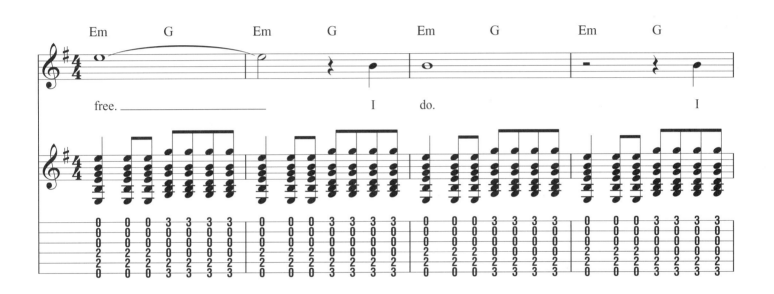

free. ___ I do. I

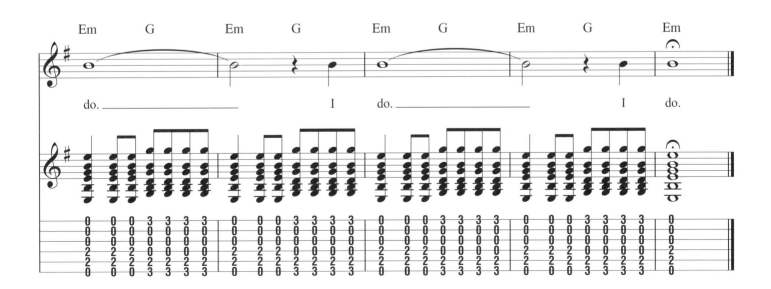

do. ___ I do. ___ I do.

Additional Lyrics

2. I'm standing in your line,
   I do, hope you have the time.
   I do, pick a number to,
   I do, keep a date with you.

Babe, I'm Gonna Leave You

Words and Music by Anne Bredon, Jimmy Page and Robert Plant

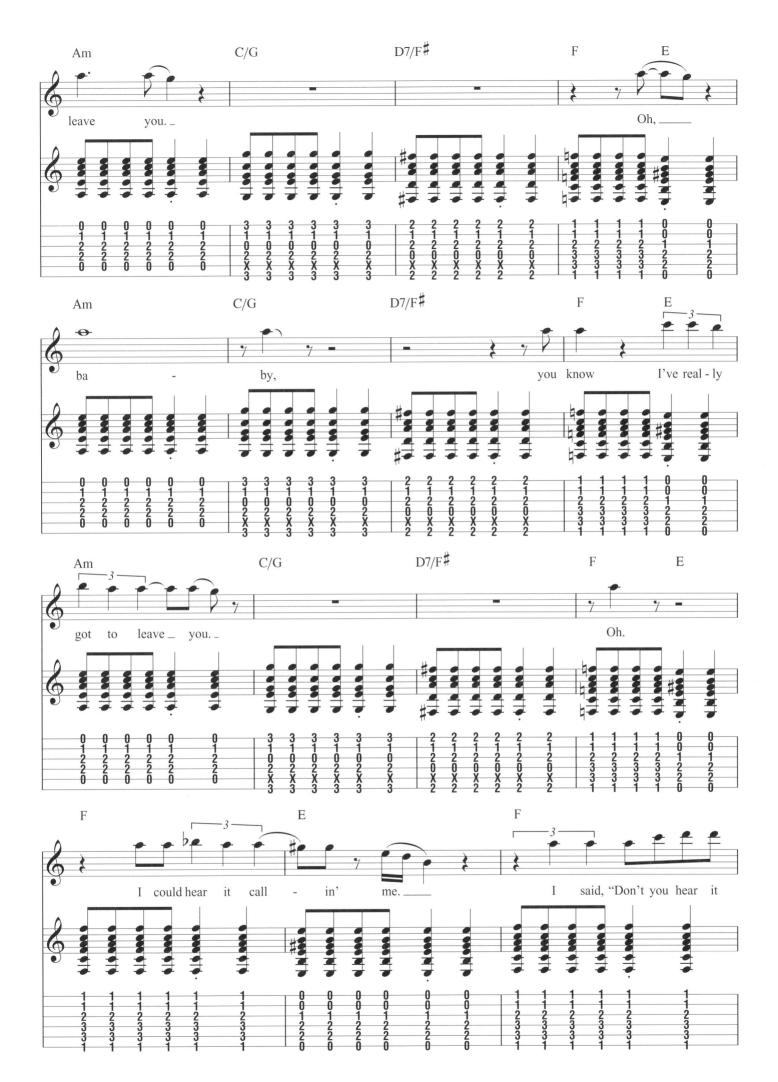

Interlude

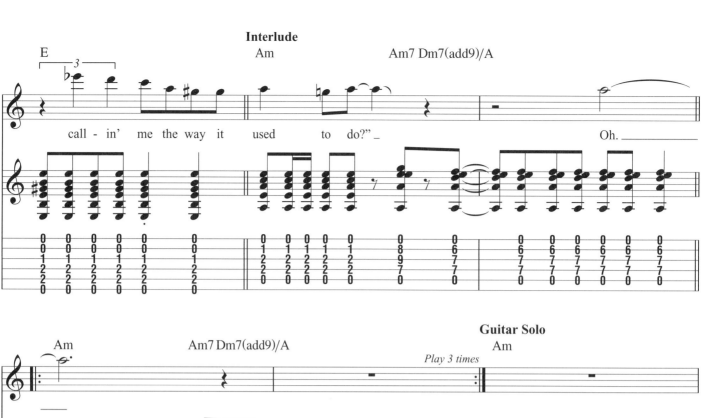

call - in' me the way it used to do?" _ Oh. _____

Guitar Solo

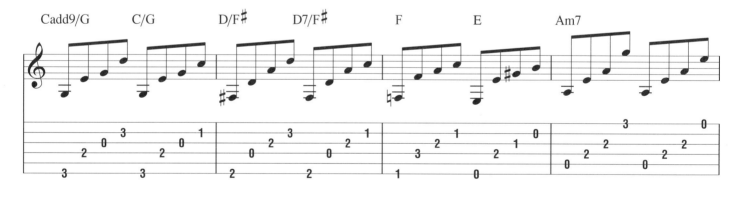

Play 3 times

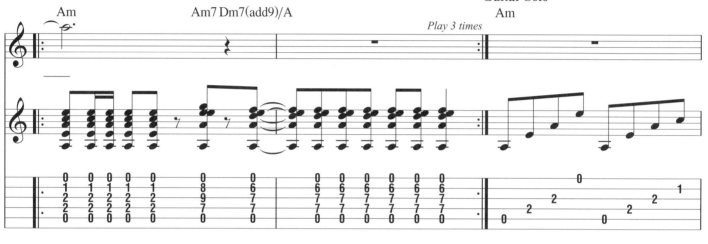

Verse

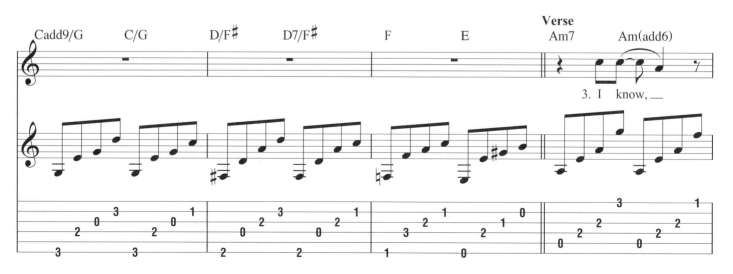

3. I know, _

14

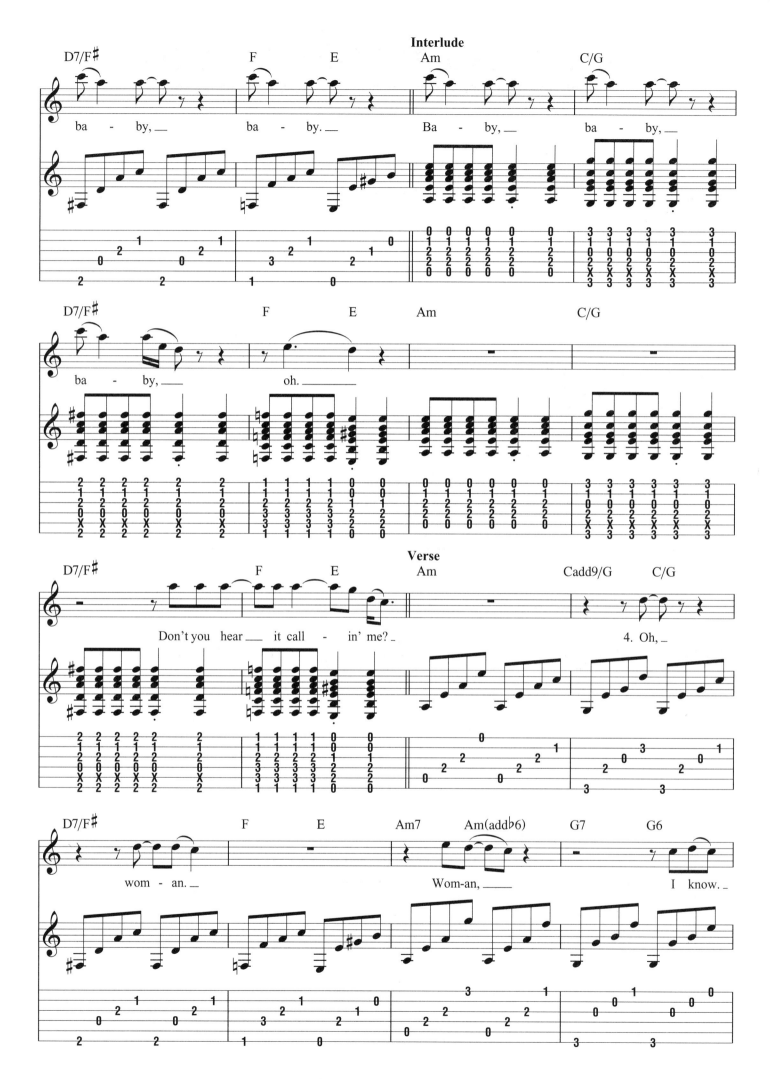

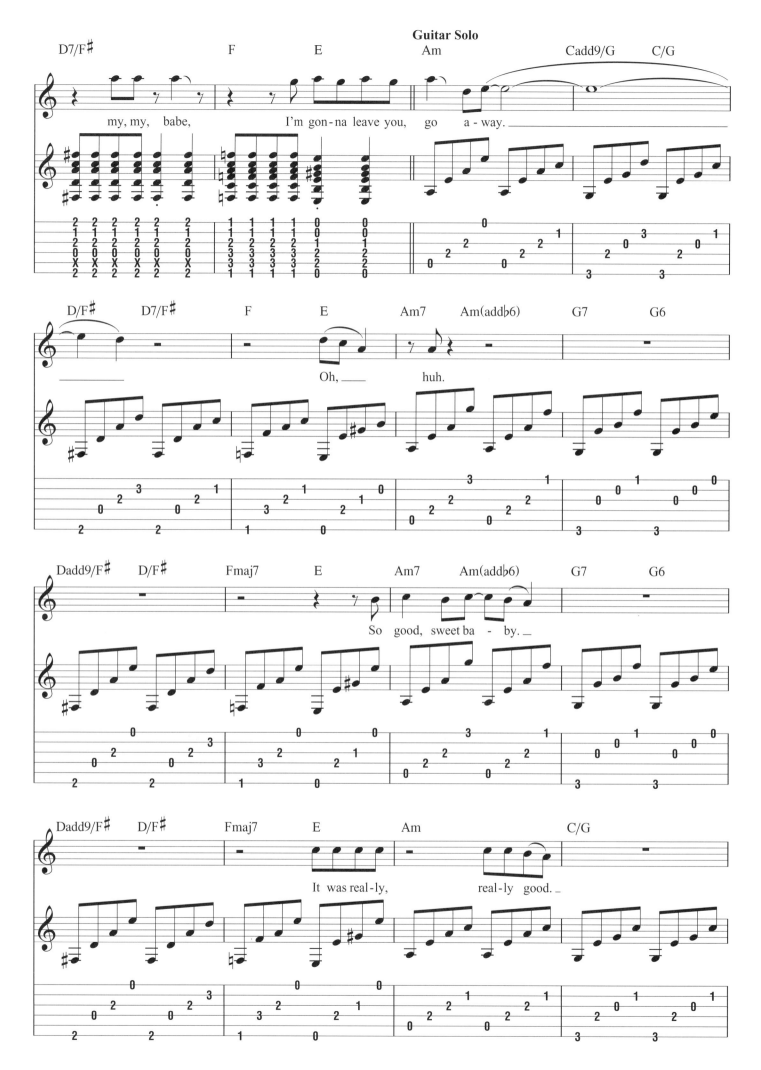

Breaking the Girl

Words and Music by Anthony Kiedis, Flea, John Frusciante and Chad Smith

Tune down 1/2 step:
(low to high) E♭-A♭-D♭-G♭-B♭-E♭

Intro
Moderately ♩. = 60

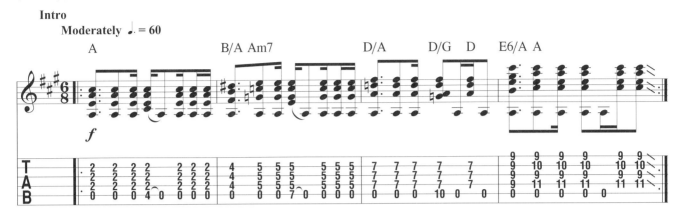

1. I _____ am a man _____ cut from _____ the know.
2. *See additional lyrics*

Rare - ly do friends _____ come and _____ then go. _____

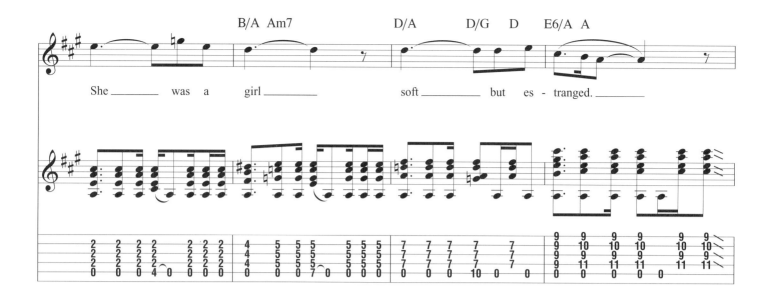

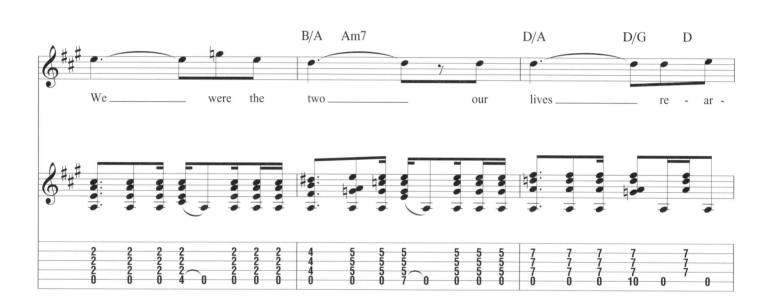

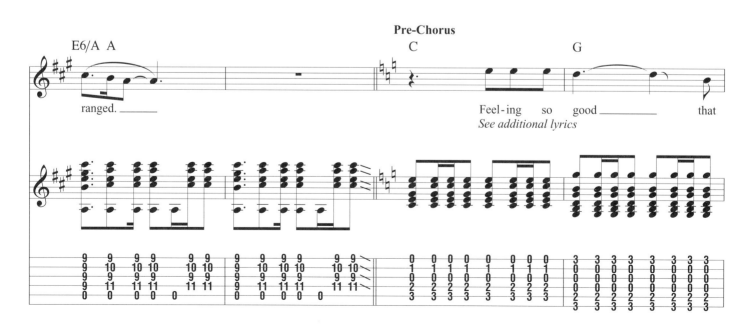

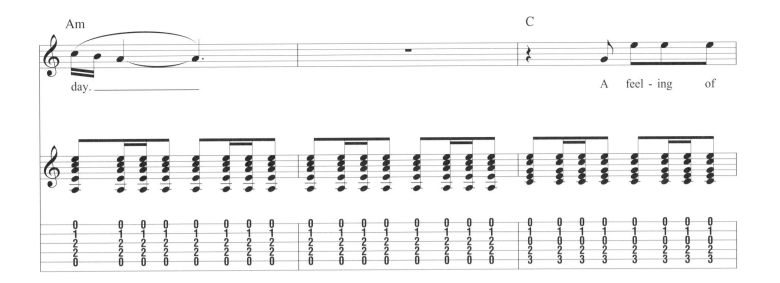

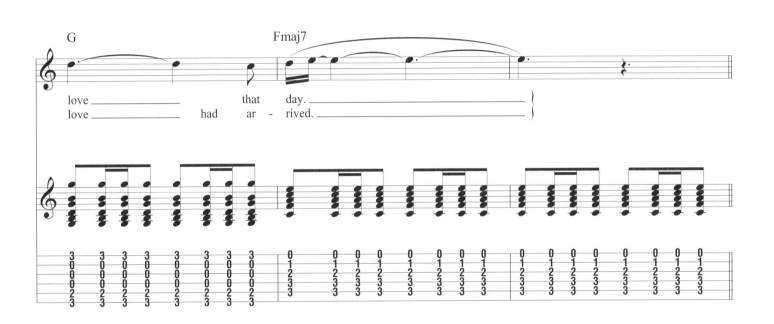

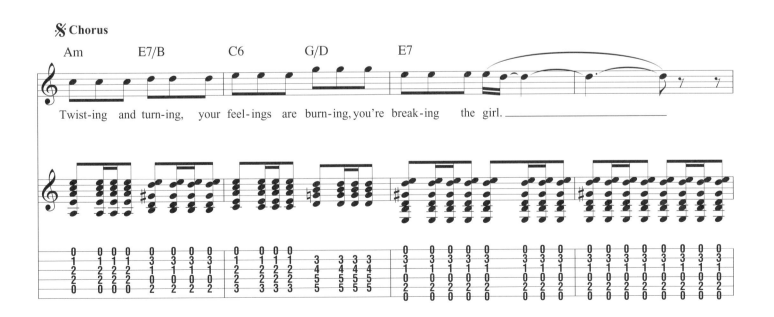

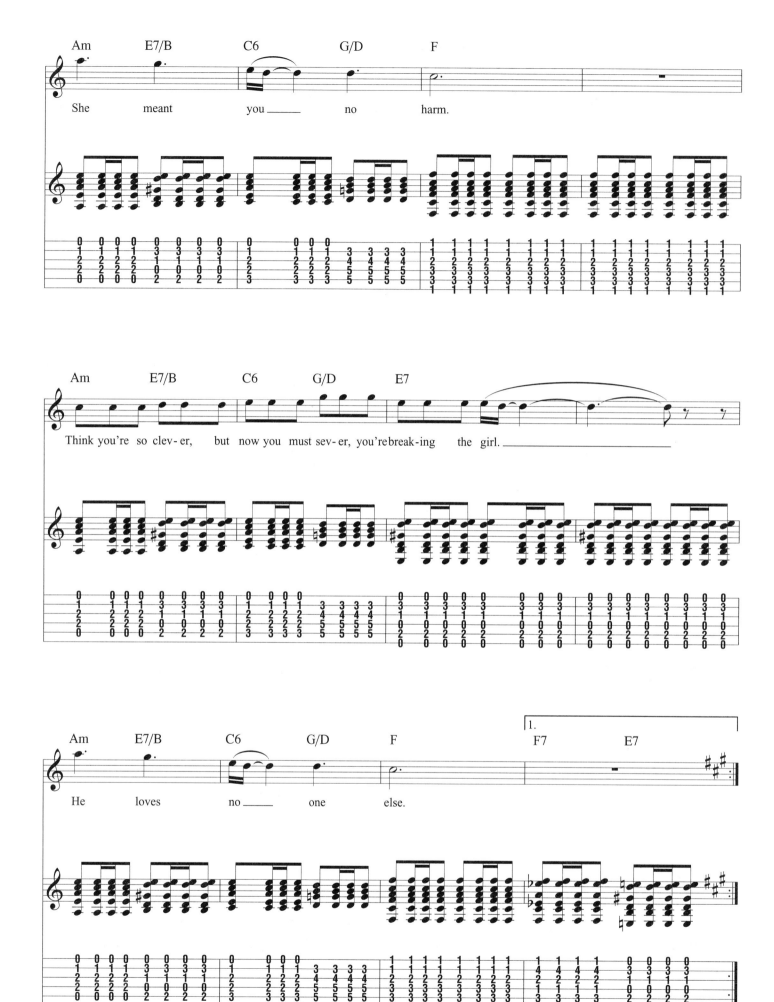

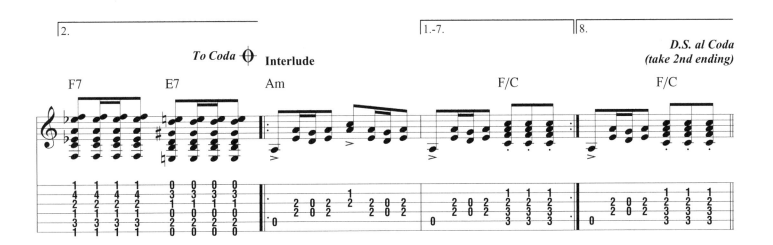

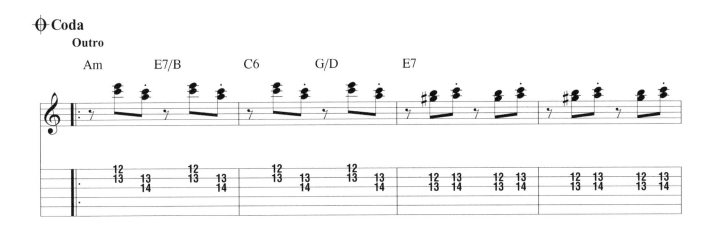

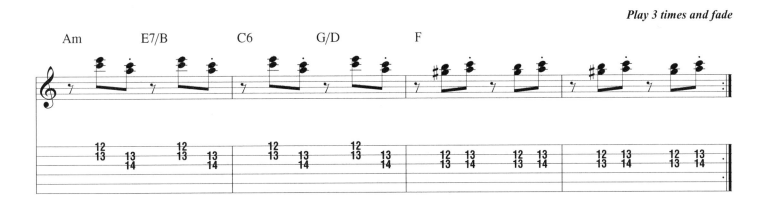

Additional Lyrics

2. Raised by my dad, girl of the day.
   He was my man, that was the way.
   She was the girl left alone.
   Feeling no need to make me her home.

Pre-Chorus I don't know what, when or why.
           The twilight of love had arrived.

Free Fallin'

Words and Music by Tom Petty and Jeff Lynne

Intro
Moderately slow ♩ = 84

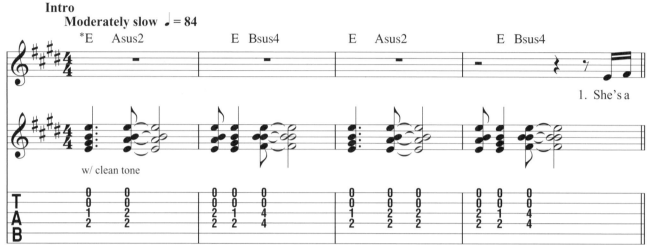

*To match original recording, place capo at 1st fret.

Verse

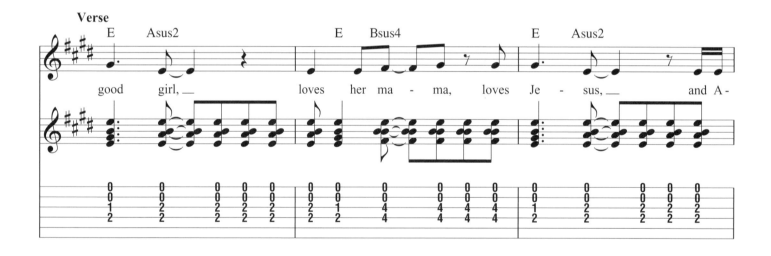

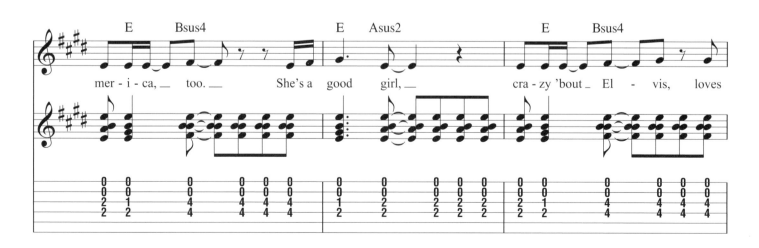

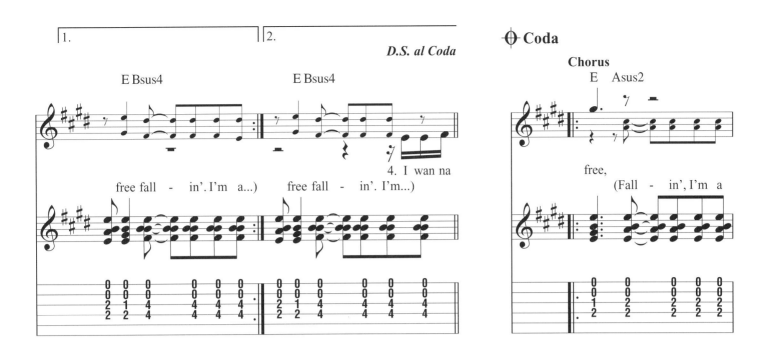

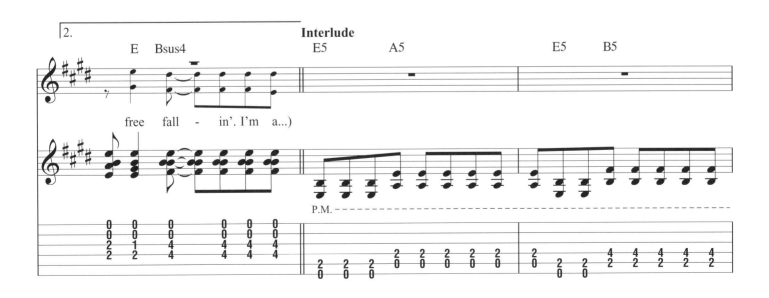

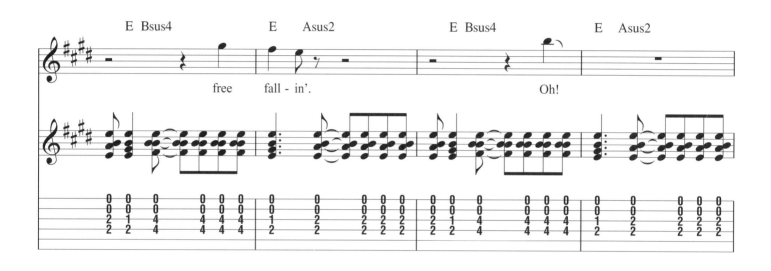

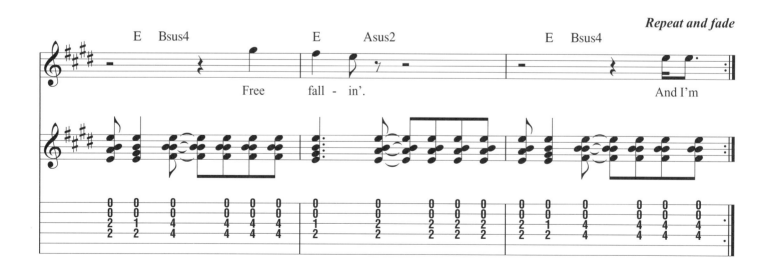

Additional Lyrics

3. Now all the vampires walkin' through the valley
   Move west down Ventura Boulevard.
   And all the bad boys are standin' in the shadows,
   And the good girls are home with broken hearts.

4. I wanna glide down over Mulholland,
   I wanna write her name in the sky.
   I'm gonna free fall out into nothin',
   Gonna leave this world for a while.

I'm Yours

Words and Music by Jason Mraz

Mm, _____ mm, hmm, _____ mm.

2. Well, o - pen up your mind and see _____ like me. _____

O - pen up your plans and, damn, _____ you're free.

Verse

Verse

Good Riddance
(Time of Your Life)

Words by Billie Joe
Music by Green Day

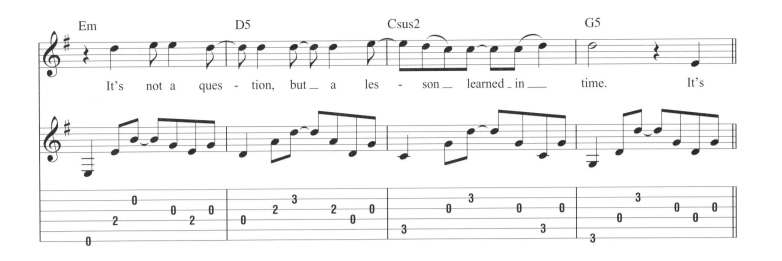

It's not a ques - tion, but _ a les - son _ learned _ in ____ time. It's

Chorus

some-thing un - pre - dict - a - ble, _ but in the end _ is right. ___ I

Interlude

hope you had _ the time _____ of _ your life. ___

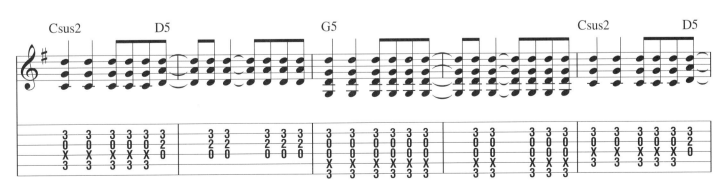

Verse

2. So take the pho - to - graphs _ and still _ frames in _ your _

mind.   Hang _ it   on _ a _ shelf _ in   good _ health and _ good _

time.   Tat - toos   of mem - o - ries, _ and   dead _____ skin _ on   trial. _

_____   For what it's   worth, _ it _ was   worth _____ all _ the _

Chorus

while.   It's some-thing un - pre - dict - a - ble, ___   but

in the end ___ is right. ___ I hope you had ___ the time _____ of ___ your life. ___

Interlude

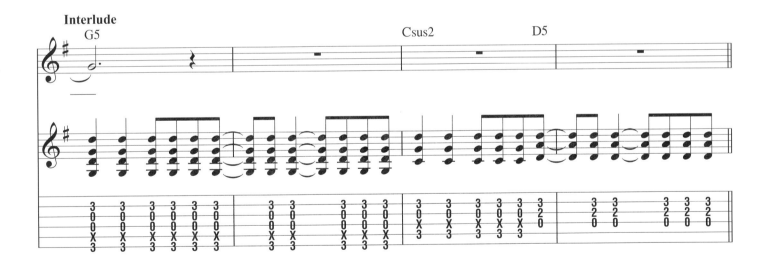

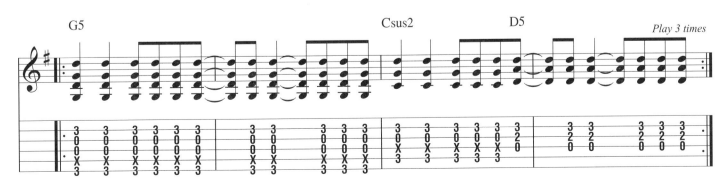

Play 3 times

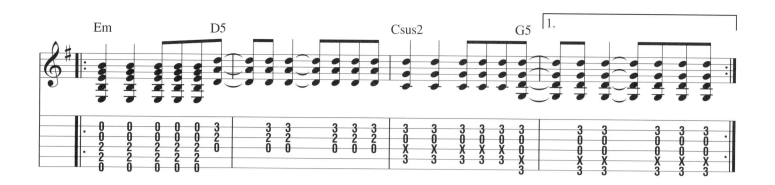

2.   **Chorus**

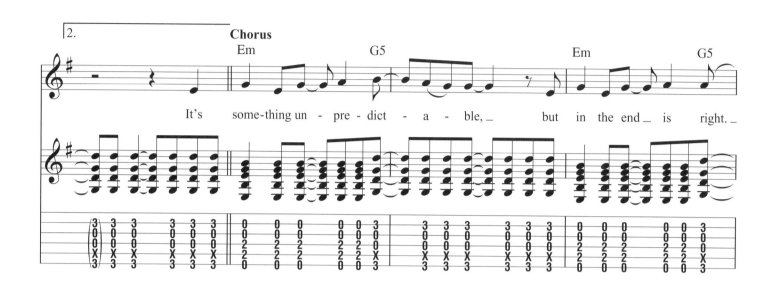

It's some-thing un - pre - dict - a - ble, _ but in the end _ is right. _

_ I hope you had _ the time _____ of _ your life. _

Interlude

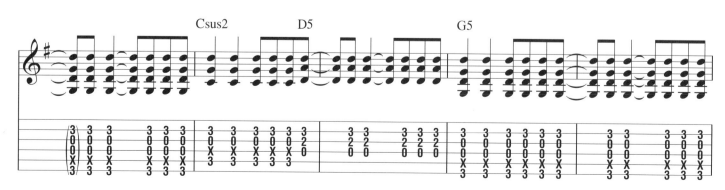

46

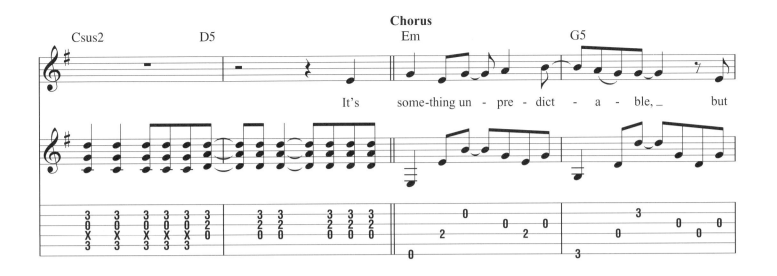

It's some-thing un - pre - dict - a - ble,_ but

in the end_ is right._ I hope you had_ the time __ of_ your life._

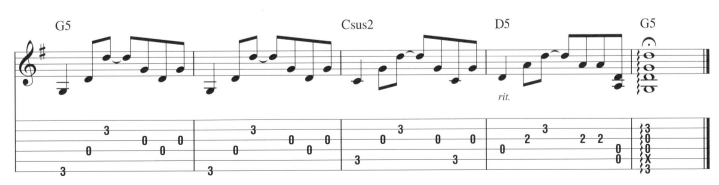

Norwegian Wood (This Bird Has Flown)

Words and Music by John Lennon and Paul McCartney

Capo II

Intro

Moderately ♩ = 64

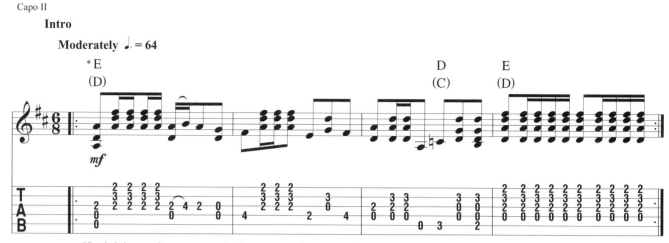

*Symbols in parentheses represent chord names respective to capoed guitar.
Symbols above reflect actual sounding chords. Capoed fret is "0" in tab.

Verse

1. I once had a girl, or should I say she once had

me. She showed me her room, is-n't it

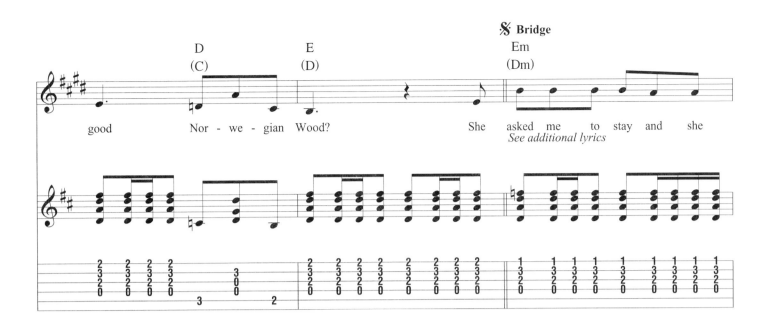

D
(C)

E
(D)

𝄋 **Bridge**

Em
(Dm)

good   Nor - we - gian Wood?   She   asked   me   to   stay   and   she
See additional lyrics

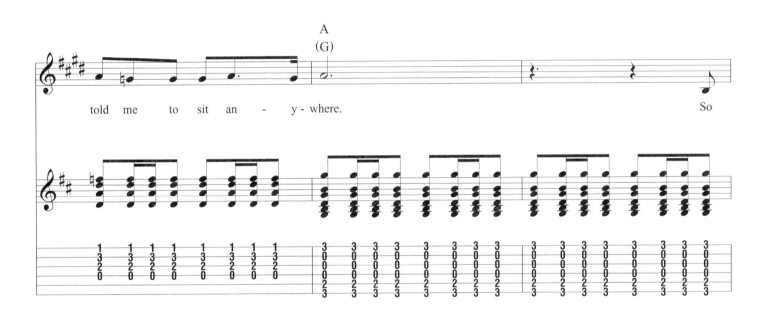

A
(G)

told   me   to   sit   an   -   y - where.   So

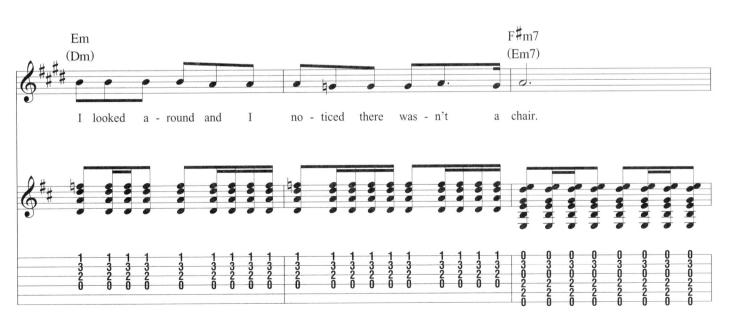

Em
(Dm)

F#m7
(Em7)

I   looked   a - round   and   I   no - ticed   there   was - n't   a   chair.

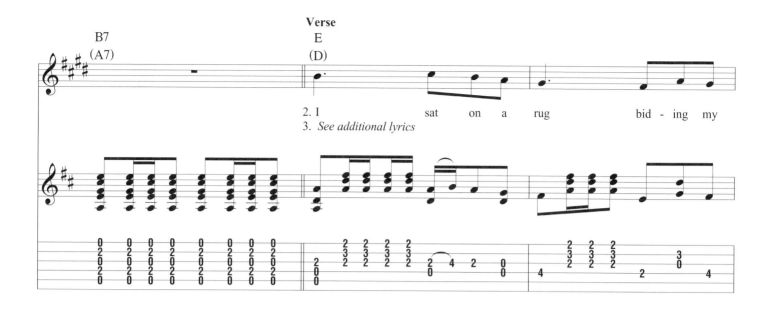

Verse

2. I sat on a rug bid - ing my
3. *See additional lyrics*

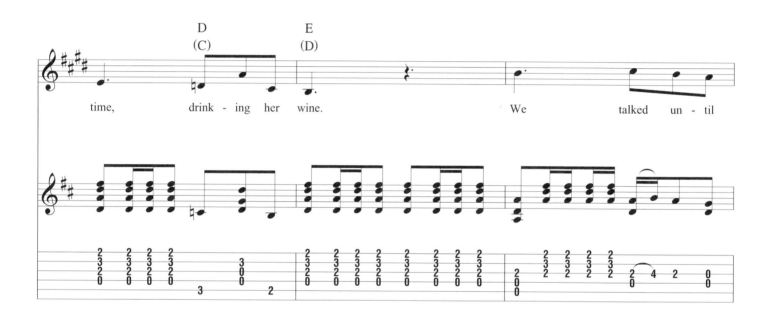

time, drink - ing her wine. We talked un - til

To Coda ⊕

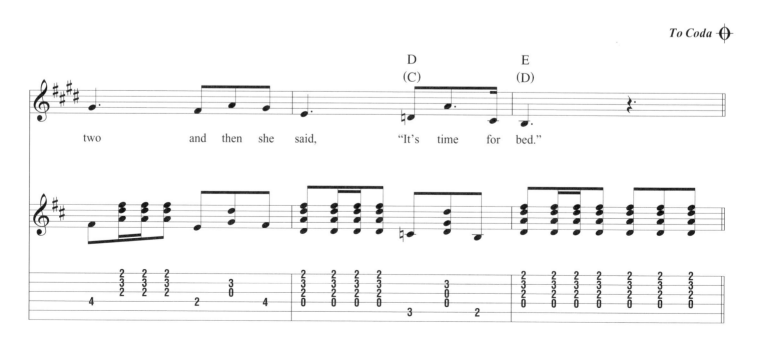

two and then she said, "It's time for bed."

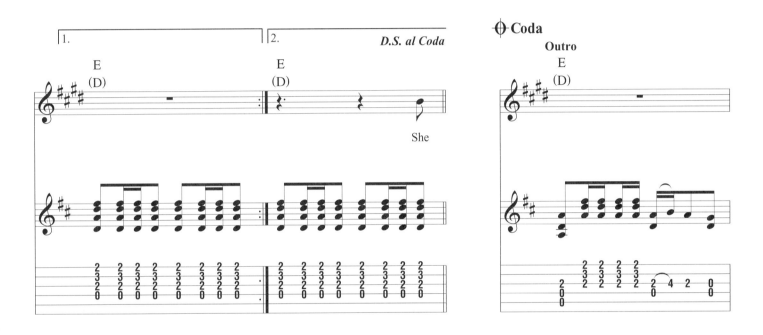

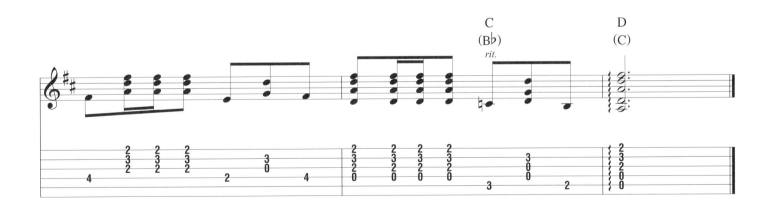

Additional Lyrics

Bridge She told me she worked in the morning and started to laugh.
I told her I didn't and crawled off to sleep in the bath.

3. And when I awoke I was alone; this bird had flown.
So, I lit a fire. Isn't it good Norwegian Wood?

The Scientist

Words and Music by Guy Berryman, Jon Buckland, Will Champion and Chris Martin

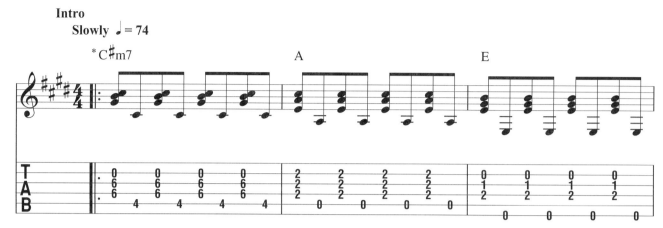

*To match original recording, place capo at 1st fret.

Verse

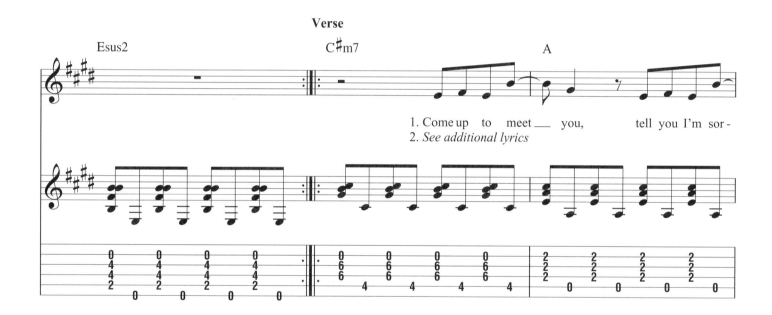

1. Come up to meet ___ you, tell you I'm sor -
2. *See additional lyrics*

- ry, you don't know how love - ly you are. ___ I had to find ___

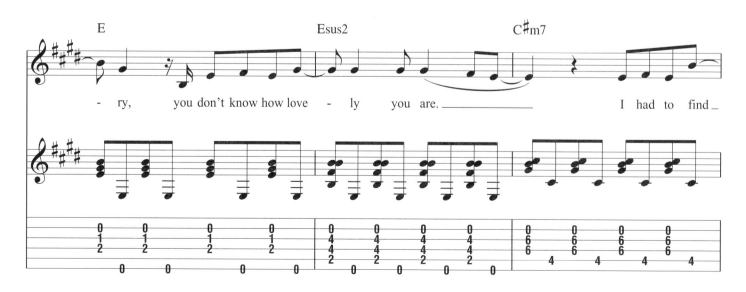

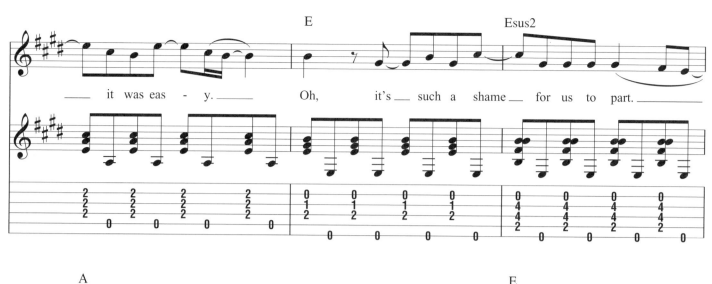

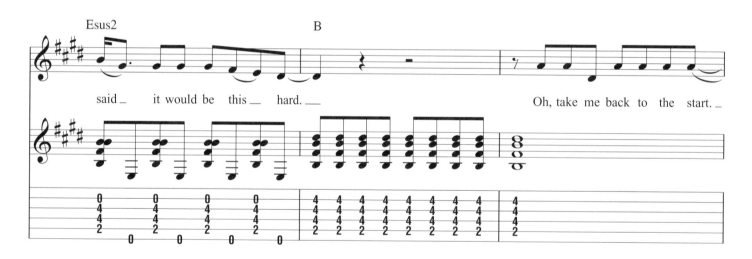

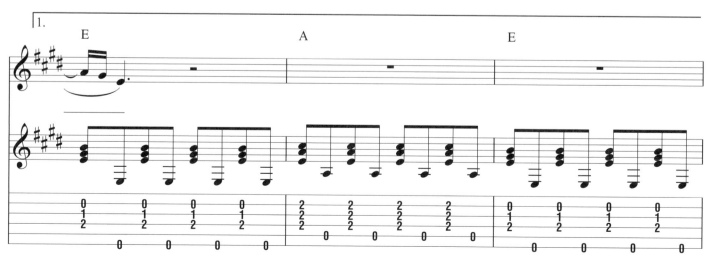

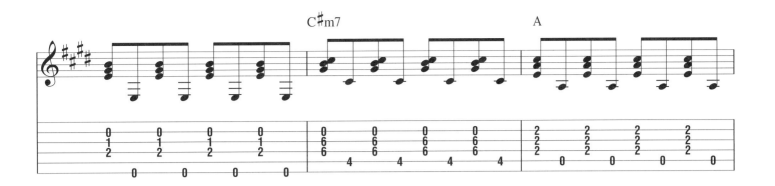

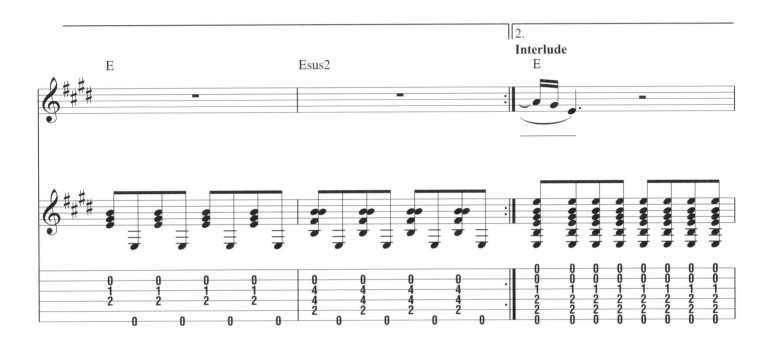

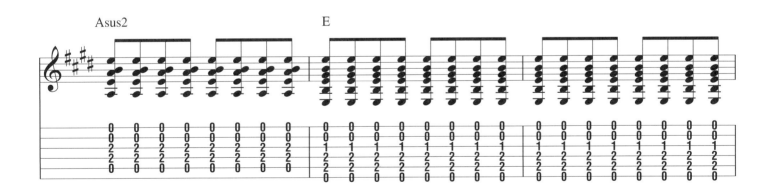

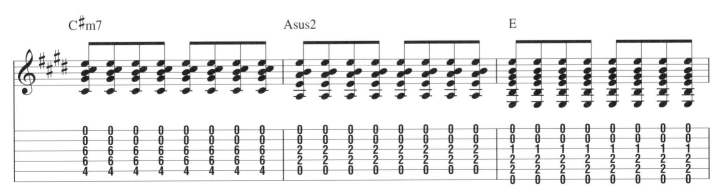

Outro

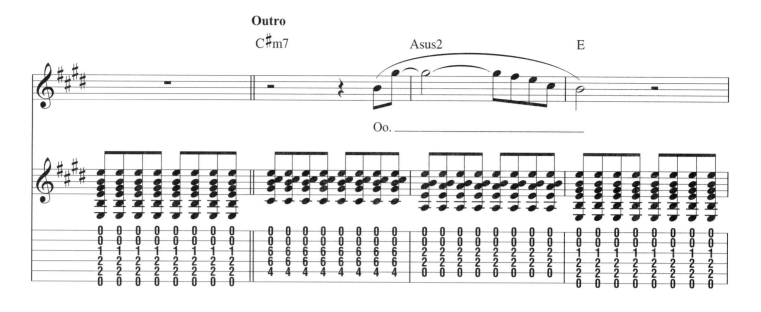

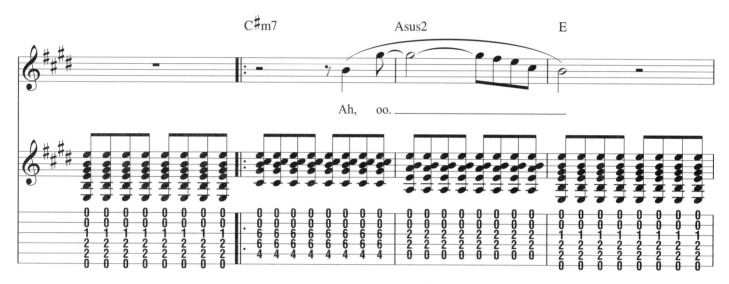

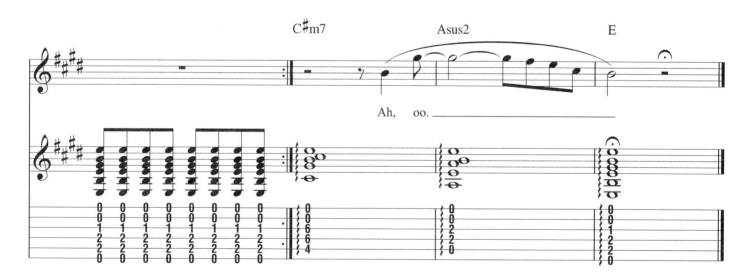

Additional Lyrics

2. I was just guessin' at numbers and figures,
Pullin' your puzzles apart.
Questions of science, science and progress
That must speak as loud as my heart.
Tell me you love me, come back and haunt me.
Oh, and I rush to the start.
Runnin' in circles, chasing our tails.
Comin' back as we are.

Tears in Heaven

Words and Music by Eric Clapton and Will Jennings

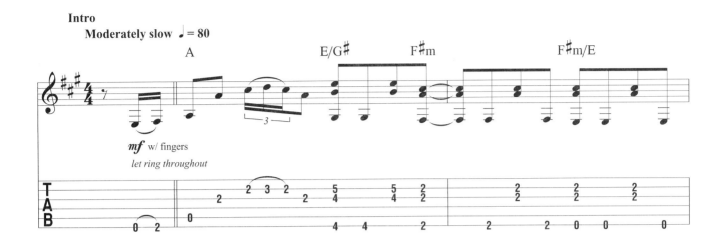

Would it be the same,_____ if I saw you in heav-

Chorus

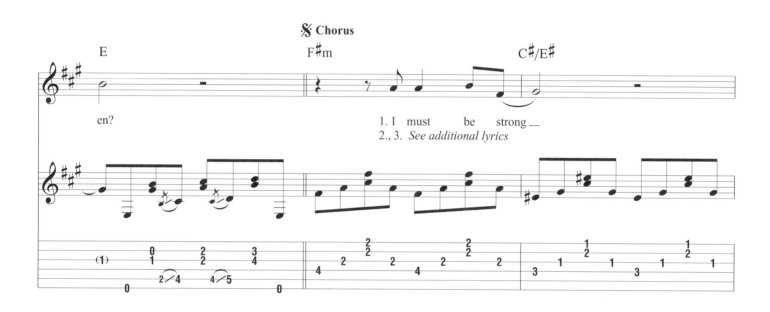

en?

1. I must be strong ___
2., 3. *See additional lyrics*

and car - ry on,_____ 'cause I know ___ I don't ___ be - long ___

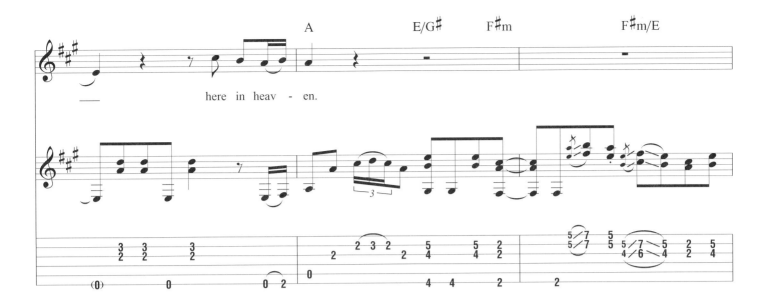

here in heav - en.

Time _ can bring   you   down, _   time can   bend _ your   knees. _

Time _ can break your heart, _ have you beg-gin' please, _

beg - gin' please. _

Guitar Solo

60

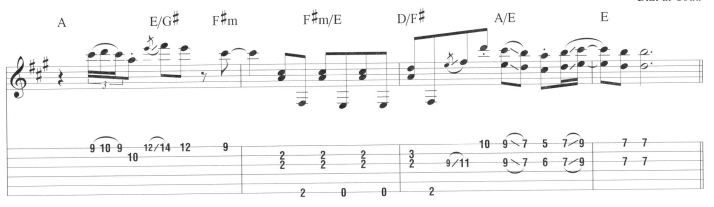

Coda

if I saw you in heav - en?

Chorus

I must be strong __ and car - ry on, ___ 'cause I know __

__ I don't __ be - long ___ here in heav - en,

'cause _ I know I don't _ be - long _ here in heav - en.

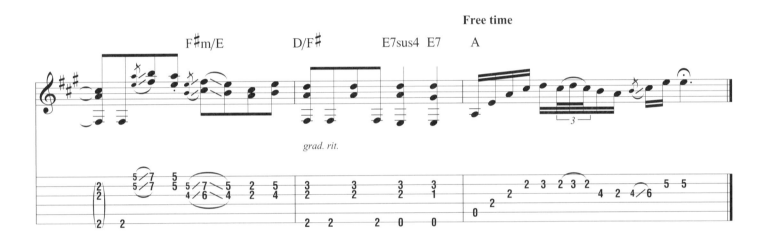

Free time

grad. rit.

Additional Lyrics

2. Would you hold my hand
   If I saw you in heaven?
   Would ya help me stand
   If I saw you in heaven?

Chorus 2. I'll find my way
   Through night and day
   'Cause I know I just can't stay
   Here in heaven.

Chorus 3. Beyond the door
   There's peace, I'm sure,
   And I know there'll be no more
   Tears in heaven.

Wonderwall

Words and Music by Noel Gallagher

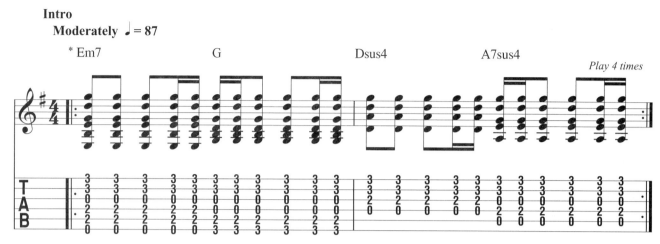

*To match original recording, place capo at 2nd fret.

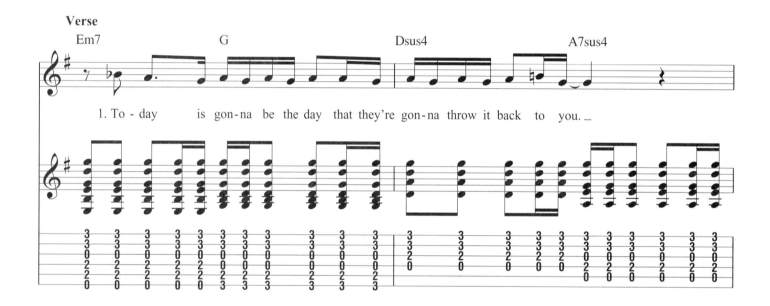

1. To - day is gon-na be the day that they're gon-na throw it back to you. __

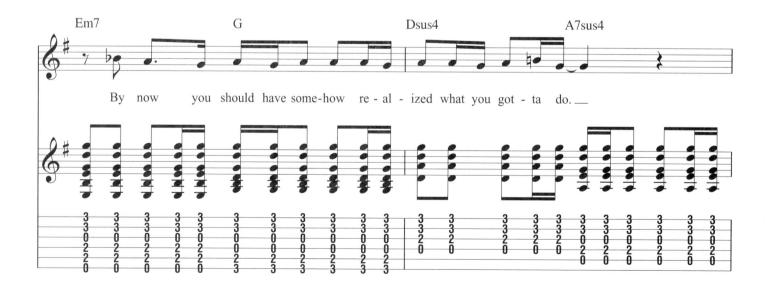

By now you should have some-how re - al - ized what you got - ta do. __

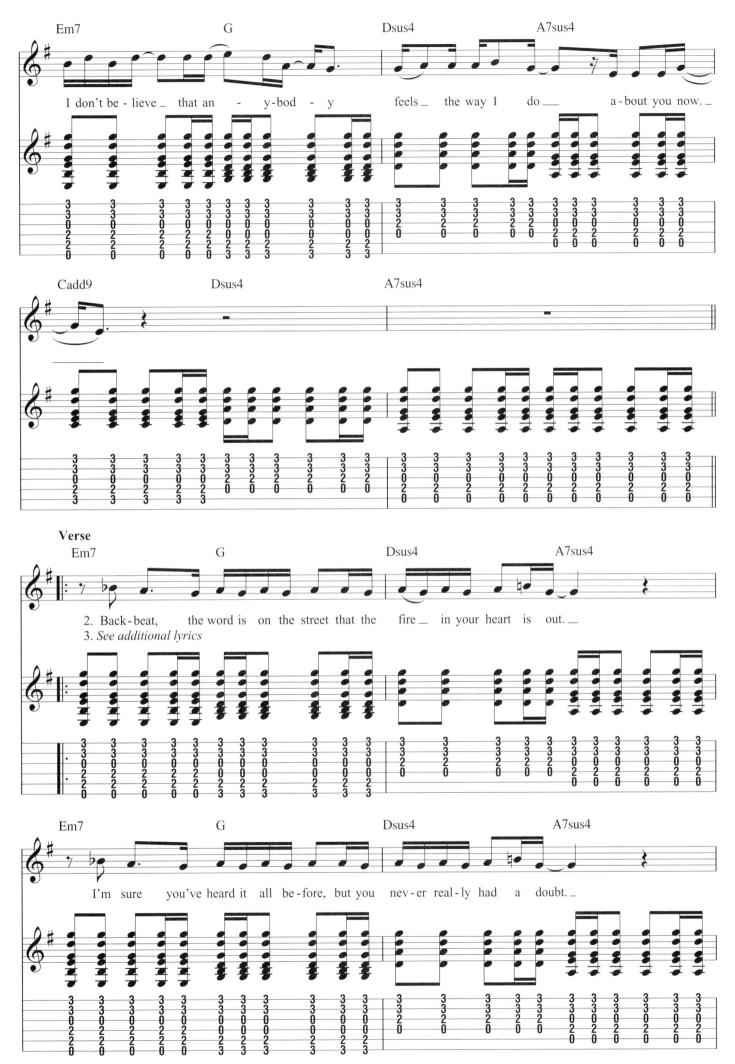

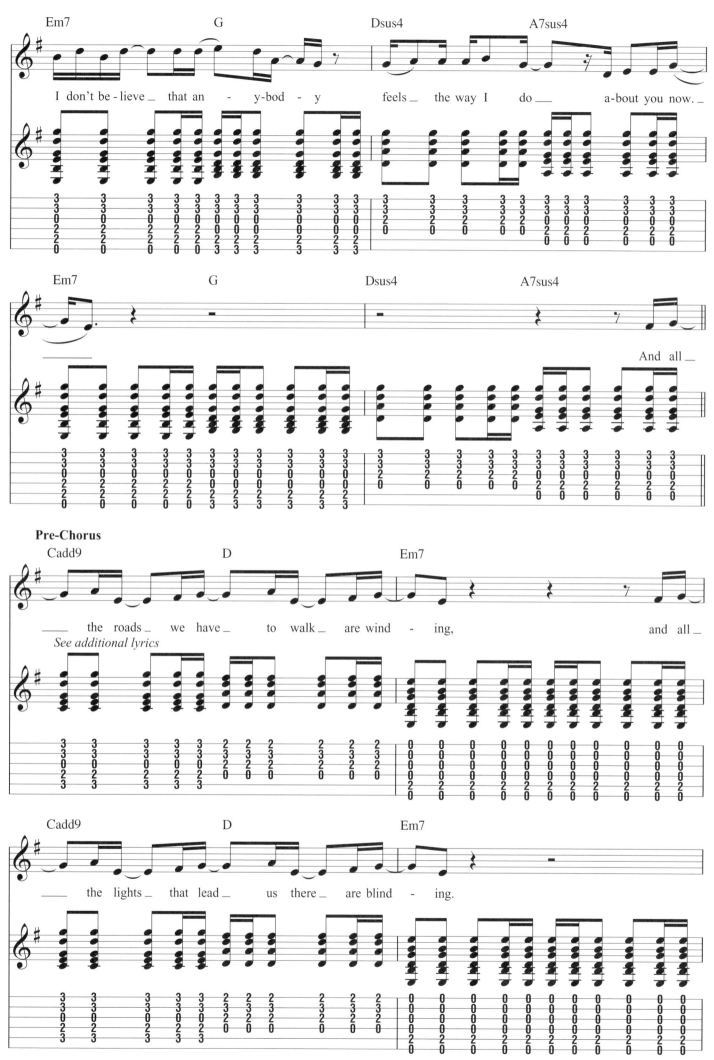

Em7   G   Dsus4   A7sus4

I don't be-lieve __ that an - y-bod - y feels __ the way I do __ a-bout you now. __

Em7   G   Dsus4   A7sus4

And all __

Pre-Chorus

Cadd9   D   Em7

__ the roads __ we have __ to walk __ are wind - ing,   and all __

See additional lyrics

Cadd9   D   Em7

__ the lights __ that lead __ us there __ are blind - ing.

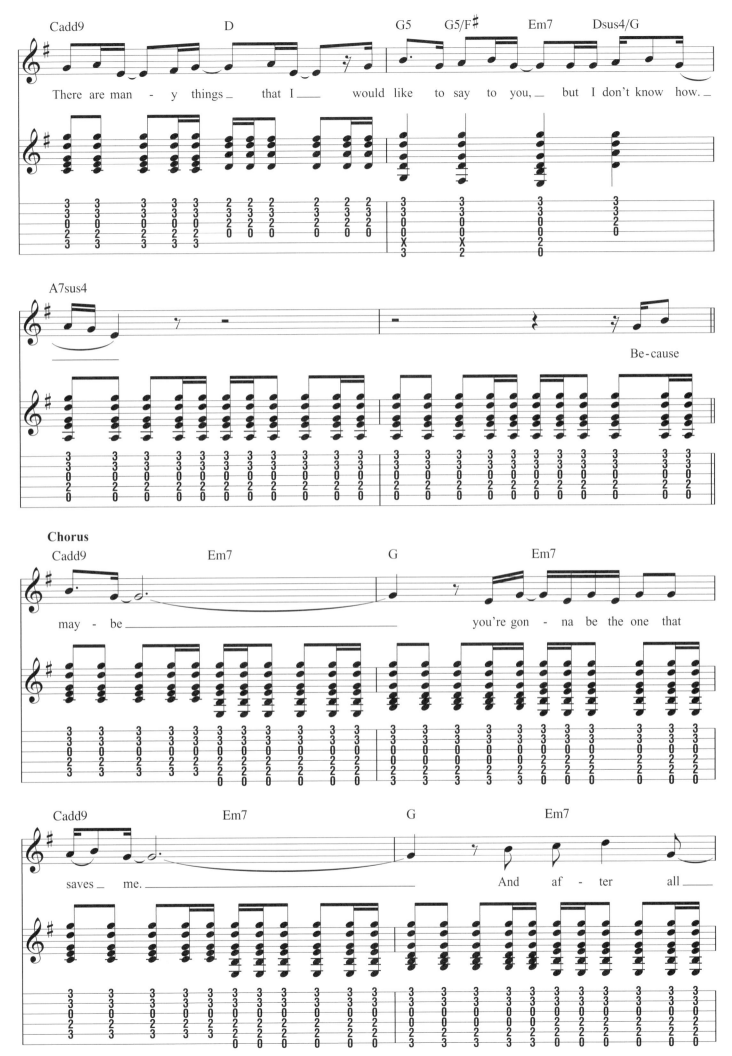

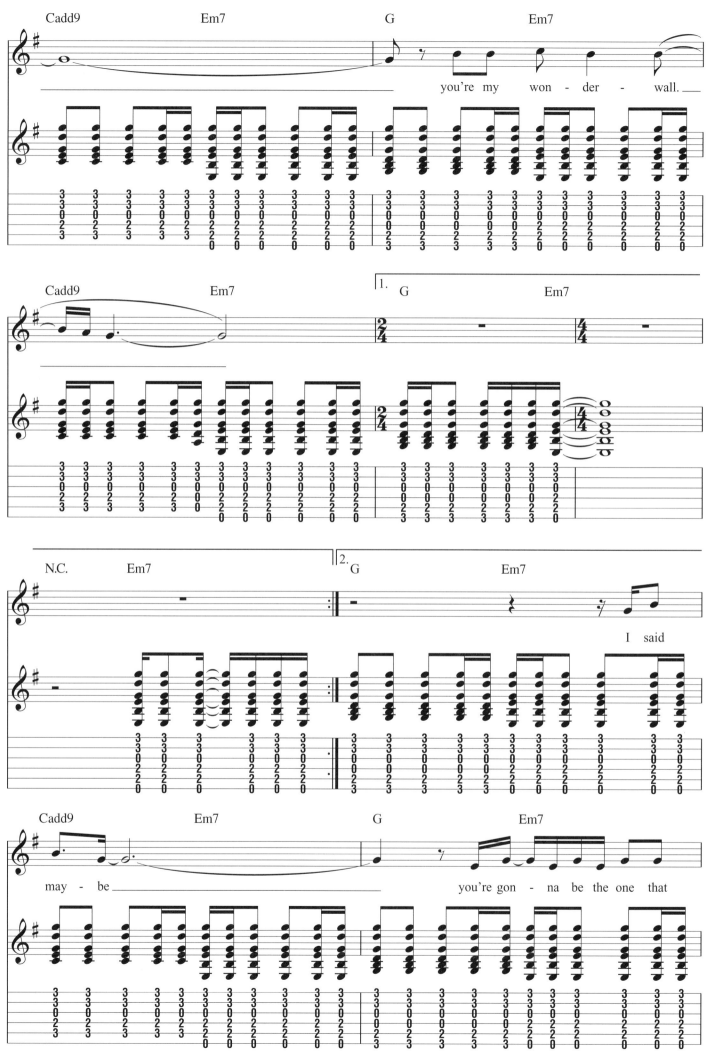

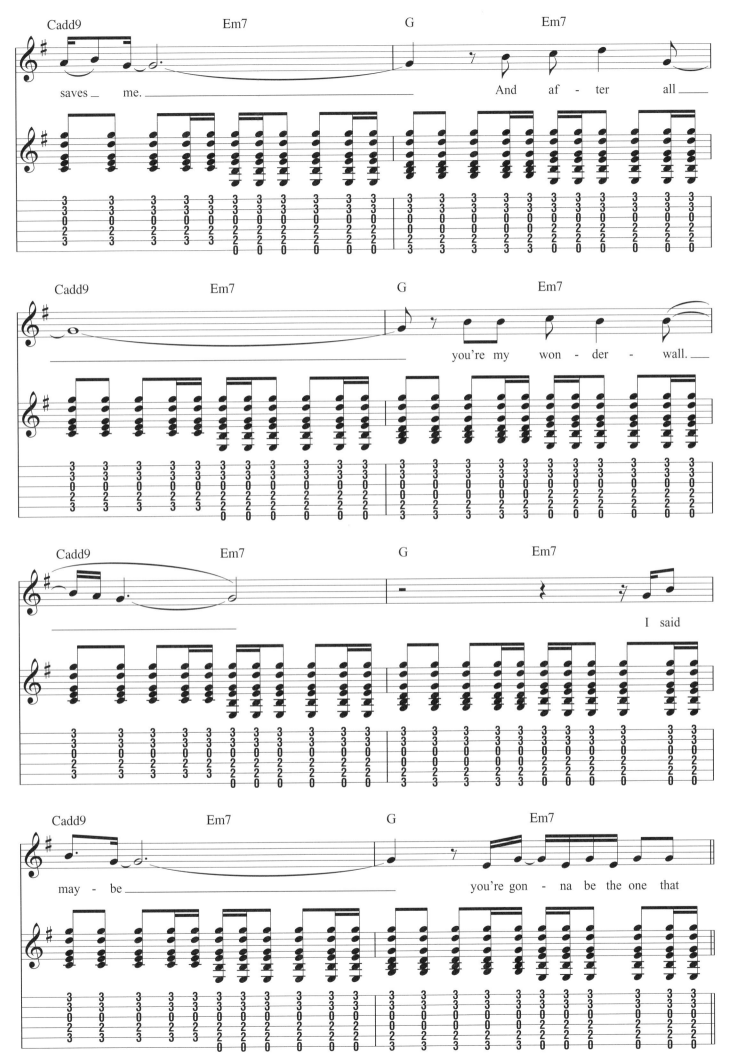

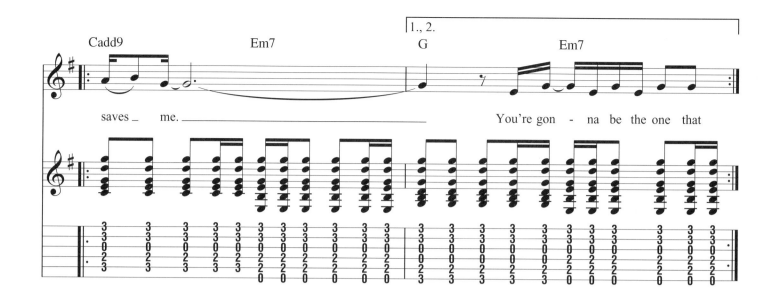

saves _ me. _____

1., 2.

You're gon - na be the one that

3.

Outro

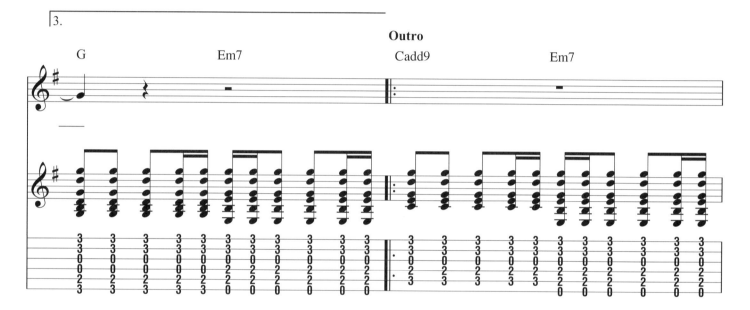

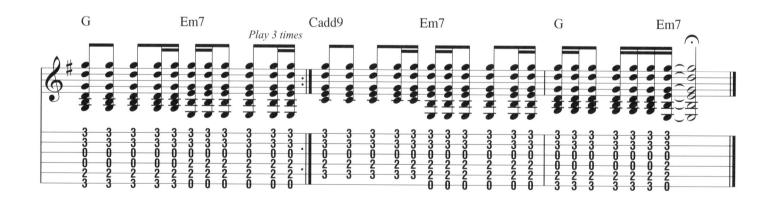

Play 3 times

Additional Lyrics

3. Today was gonna be the day, but they'll never throw it back to you.
By now you should have somehow realized what you're not to do.
I don't believe that anybody feels the way I do about you now.

Pre-Chorus 3. And all the roads that lead you there were winding,
And all the lights that light the way are blinding.
There are many things that I would like to say to you,
But I don't know how.
I said...

HAL LEONARD GUITAR METHOD

by Will Schmid and Greg Koch

THE HAL LEONARD GUITAR METHOD is designed for anyone just learning to play acoustic or electric guitar. It is based on years of teaching guitar students of all ages, and it also reflects some of the best guitar teaching ideas from around the world. This comprehensive method includes: A learning sequence carefully paced with clear instructions; popular songs which increase the incentive to learn to play; versatility – can be used as self-instruction or with a teacher; audio accompaniments so that students have fun and sound great while practicing.

BOOK 1
00699010 Book $8.99
00699027 Book with audio on CD & Online $12.99
00155480 Deluxe Beginner Pack
          (Book/DVD/CD/Online Audio &
          Video/Poster) $19.99

BOOK 2
00699020 Book $8.99
00697313 Book/CD Pack $12.99

BOOK 3
00699030 Book $8.99
00697316 Book/Online Audio $12.99

COMPOSITE
Books 1, 2, and 3 bound together in an easy-to-use spiral binding.
00699040 Books Only $16.99
00697342 Book/Online Audio $24.99

DVD
FOR THE BEGINNING ELECTRIC
OR ACOUSTIC GUITARIST
00697318 DVD $19.95
00697341 Book/CD Pack and DVD $24.99

GUITAR FOR KIDS
A BEGINNER'S GUIDE WITH STEP-BY-STEP INSTRUCTION
FOR ACOUSTIC AND ELECTRIC GUITAR
by Bob Morris and Jeff Schroedl
00865003 Book 1 – Book/Online Audio $12.99
00697402 Songbook Book/Online Audio...............$9.99
00128437 Book 2 – Book/Online Audio $12.99

SONGBOOKS

EASY POP MELODIES
00697281 Book $6.99
00697440 Book/Online Audio $14.99

MORE EASY POP MELODIES
00697280 Book $6.99
00697269 Book/Online Audio $14.99

EVEN MORE EASY POP MELODIES
00699154 Book $6.99
00697439 Book/Online Audio $14.99

EASY POP RHYTHMS
00697336 Book $7.99
00697441 Book/Online Audio $14.99

MORE EASY POP RHYTHMS
00697338 Book $7.99
00697322 Book/Online Audio $14.95

EVEN MORE EASY POP RHYTHMS
00697340 Book $7.99
00697323 Book/Online Audio $14.99

EASY SOLO GUITAR PIECES
00110407 Book $9.99

EASY POP CHRISTMAS MELODIES
00697417 Book $6.99
00697416 Book/Online Audio $14.99

LEAD LICKS
00697345 Book/Online Audio $10.99

RHYTHM RIFFS
00697346 Book/Online Audio $10.99

STYLISTIC METHODS

ACOUSTIC GUITAR
00697347 Book/Online Audio $16.99
00697384 Acoustic Guitar Songs $15.99

BLUEGRASS GUITAR
00697405 Book/CD Pack $16.99

BLUES GUITAR
00697326 Book/Online Audio $16.99
00697385 Blues Guitar Songs
          (with Online Audio)..............................$14.99

BRAZILIAN GUITAR
00697415 Book/Online Audio $14.99

CHRISTIAN GUITAR
00695947 Book/CD Pack $12.99
00697408 Christian Guitar Songs........................$14.99

CLASSICAL GUITAR
00697376 Book/Online Audio $14.99
00697388 Classical Guitar Pieces $9.99

COUNTRY GUITAR
00697337 Book/Online Audio $22.99
00697400 Country Guitar Songs $14.99

FINGERSTYLE GUITAR
00697378 Book/Online Audio $19.99
00697432 Fingerstyle Guitar Songs
          (with Online Audio)..............................$14.99

FLAMENCO GUITAR
00697363 Book/Online Audio $14.99

FOLK GUITAR
00697414 Book/Online Audio $14.99

JAZZ GUITAR
00695359 Book/Online Audio $19.99
00697386 Jazz Guitar Songs $14.95

JAZZ-ROCK FUSION
00697387 Book/Online Audio $19.99

ROCK GUITAR
00697319 Book/Online Audio $16.99
00697383 Rock Guitar Songs $14.95

ROCKABILLY GUITAR
00697407 Book/Online Audio $16.99

R&B GUITAR
00697356 Book/CD Pack $16.99
00697433 R&B Guitar Songs $14.99

REFERENCE

ARPEGGIO FINDER
00697351 9" x 12" Edition $6.99

INCREDIBLE CHORD FINDER
00697200 6" x 9" Edition $6.99
00697208 9" x 12" Edition $6.99

INCREDIBLE SCALE FINDER
00695568 6" x 9" Edition $5.99
00695490 9" x 12" Edition $6.99

GUITAR CHORD, SCALE & ARPEGGIO FINDER
00697410...$19.99

GUITAR SETUP & MAINTENANCE
00697427 6" x 9" Edition $14.99
00697421 9" x 12" Edition $12.99

GUITAR TECHNIQUES
00697389 Book/CD Pack $12.95

GUITAR PRACTICE PLANNER
00697401...$5.99

MUSIC THEORY FOR GUITARISTS
00695790 Book/Online Audio $19.99

HAL•LEONARD®

www.halleonard.com

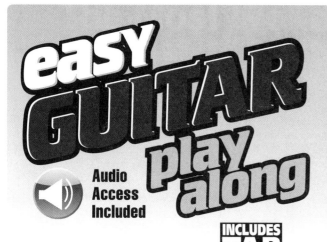

Audio Access Included

INCLUDES TAB

The *Easy Guitar Play Along* ® series features streamlined transcriptions of your favorite songs. Just follow the tab, listen to the audio to hear how the guitar should sound, and then play along using the backing tracks. Playback tools are provided for slowing down the tempo without changing pitch and looping challenging parts. The melody and lyrics are included in the book so that you can sing or simply follow along.

1. ROCK CLASSICS
Jailbreak • Living After Midnight • Mississippi Queen • Rocks Off • Runnin' Down a Dream • Smoke on the Water • Strutter • Up Around the Bend.
00702560 Book/CD Pack....... $14.99

2. ACOUSTIC TOP HITS
About a Girl • I'm Yours • The Lazy Song • The Scientist • 21 Guns • Upside Down • What I Got • Wonderwall.
00702569 Book/CD Pack....... $14.99

3. ROCK HITS
All the Small Things • Best of You • Brain Stew (The Godzilla Remix) • Californication • Island in the Sun • Plush • Smells Like Teen Spirit • Use Somebody.
00702570 Book/CD Pack....... $14.99

4. ROCK 'N' ROLL
Blue Suede Shoes • I Get Around • I'm a Believer • Jailhouse Rock • Oh, Pretty Woman • Peggy Sue • Runaway • Wake Up Little Susie.
00702572 Book/CD Pack....... $14.99

6. CHRISTMAS SONGS
Have Yourself a Merry Little Christmas • A Holly Jolly Christmas • The Little Drummer Boy • Run Rudolph Run • Santa Claus Is Comin' to Town • Silver and Gold • Sleigh Ride • Winter Wonderland.
00101879 Book/CD Pack......... $14.99

7. BLUES SONGS FOR BEGINNERS
Come On (Part 1) • Double Trouble • Gangster of Love • I'm Ready • Let Me Love You Baby • Mary Had a Little Lamb • San-Ho-Zay • T-Bone Shuffle.
00103235 Book/CD Pack........ $14.99

8. ACOUSTIC SONGS FOR BEGINNERS
Barely Breathing • Drive • Everlong • Good Riddance (Time of Your Life) • Hallelujah • Hey There Delilah • Lake of Fire • Photograph.
00103240 Book/CD Pack $14.99

9. ROCK SONGS FOR BEGINNERS
Are You Gonna Be My Girl • Buddy Holly • Everybody Hurts • In Bloom • Otherside • The Rock Show • Santa Monica • When I Come Around.
00103255 Book/CD Pack.....$14.99

10. GREEN DAY
Basket Case • Boulevard of Broken Dreams • Good Riddance (Time of Your Life) • Holiday • Longview • 21 Guns • Wake Me up When September Ends • When I Come Around.
00122322 Book/CD Pack $14.99

11. NIRVANA
All Apologies • Come As You Are • Heart Shaped Box • Lake of Fire • Lithium • The Man Who Sold the World • Rape Me • Smells Like Teen Spirit.
00122325 Book/
Online Audio $14.99

12. TAYLOR SWIFT
Fifteen • Love Story • Mean • Picture to Burn • Red • We Are Never Ever Getting Back Together • White Horse • You Belong with Me.
00122326 Book/CD Pack $16.99

13. AC/DC
Back in Black • Dirty Deeds Done Dirt Cheap • For Those About to Rock (We Salute You) • Hells Bells • Highway to Hell • Rock and Roll Ain't Noise Pollution • T.N.T. • You Shook Me All Night Long.
14042895 Book/
Online Audio........$16.99

14. JIMI HENDRIX – SMASH HITS
All Along the Watchtower • Can You See Me • Crosstown Traffic • Fire • Foxey Lady • Hey Joe • Manic Depression • Purple Haze • Red House • Remember • Stone Free • The Wind Cries Mary.
00130591 Book/
Online Audio........$24.99

HAL•LEONARD ®
www.halleonard.com

Prices, contents, and availability subject to change without notice.